ELVIS PRESLEY'S HIPS & MICK JAGGER'S LIPS

Susana H. Case

ANAPHORA LITERARY PRESS

SHANTOU, CHINA

Anaphora Literary Press
Shantou, China
www.anaphoraliterary.com

Book design by Anna Faktorovich, Ph.D.

Edited by: Anna Faktorovich

Proofread by: Samantha Munoz

Published in 2012 by Anaphora Literary Press

Elvis Presley's Hips & Mick Jagger's Lips
Susana H. Case—1st edition.

ISBN-13: 978-1-937536-36-7
ISBN-10: 1-937536-36-X

Library of Congress Control Number: 2012955068

ELVIS PRESLEY'S HIPS & MICK JAGGER'S LIPS

SUSANA H. CASE

CONTENTS

This is dedicated to the one I love, Eric Hoffmann
I could be satisfied knowing you love me

 —The Shirelles, "Dedicated to the One I Love," 1959

Rock and roll doesn't necessarily mean a band. It doesn't mean a singer, and it doesn't mean a lyric, really. It's that question of trying to be immortal.

 —Malcolm McLaren, alternative music impresario and manager of the Sex Pistols

ACKNOWLEDGMENTS

With special thanks to fellow Poetry Dogs: Elizabeth Haukaas, Myra Malkin, and Larry Loeb, and much appreciation also to Anna Faktorovich and Samantha Munoz for close reading and editorial suggestions. Additional thanks to Renae Cizek for suggesting I listen to Gear Daddies and to Ryan Conatti for doing the same with DeVotchKa.

Grateful acknowledgment is made to the following where these poems have previously appeared, sometimes in different form or with a different title:

"A Willow in Autumn" - *Poetry South*
"Absent Consciousness" - *Women Write Resistance*, Laura Madeline Wiseman, ed., Blue Light Press
"Ambrosia" - *Cloudbank*
"Bizarre Love Triangle" - *Inkwell*
"Blank Beauty" - *Slices of the Apple: Voices from the New York Performance Poetry Circuit*, Spiny Babbler
"Demolished World" - *The Cortland Review*
"Give Me Money" - *Gambling the Aisle*
"He Needs a Wealthy Woman" - *Bluestem*
"It's All I Love It's All I Hate" - *The Dos Passos Review*
"Kissing Cold Air" - *Spillway*
"Motown Marvelous" - *Eclipse*
"Murdered by a Melody" - *Poetry South*
"Synonyms of Fiction" - *Red Mountain Review*
"The Crowd That Was Sedated" - *Edison Literary Review*
"The Only One She Found" - *Hawai'i Pacific Review*
"The Story's Always the Same" - *Georgetown Review* & *Anthropologist In Ohio*, Main Street Rag Publishing Company
"There's Someone in My Head but It's Not Me" - *Slant*
"They Come In Sweet and They Go Out Cold" - *Saranac Review*
"Tomorrow Isn't to the Right" - *Cider Press Review*
"Volcano Girl" - *Spillway*
"With Me, You Can Get What You Want" - *Santa Fe Literary Review*

GUIDE TO COVER ART

"The Beatles in America" By United Press International, photographer unknown [Public domain], via Wikimedia Commons.

"Florence and the Machine" By Fabio Venni from London, UK (Florence & The Machine) [CC-BY-SA-2.0 (http://creativecommons.org/licenses/by-sa/2.0)], via Wikimedia Commons.

"The Ronettes" By General Artists Corporation-GAC (management)-photographer-James Kriegsmann, New York. (eBay item photo front photo back) [Public domain], via Wikimedia Commons.

"The Marvelettes" By Motown/Tamla Records-photographer-James Kriegsmann, New York (Billboard page 13) [Public domain], via Wikimedia Commons.

"The Rolling Stones" By London Records. (Billboard page 25 1 May 1965) [Public domain], via Wikimedia Commons.

"Jefferson Airplane" By RCA Records/photographer: Herb Greene (eBay item photo front photo back) [Public domain], via Wikimedia Commons.

"Jimi Hendrix Experience" By Warner/Reprise Records Uploaded by We hope at en.wikipedia [Public domain], via Wikimedia Commons.

"The Who" By Decca Records [Public domain], via Wikimedia Commons.

"B. B. King" By Heinrich Klaffs [CC-BY-SA-1.0 (http://creativecommons.org/licenses/by-sa/1.0)], via Wikimedia Commons.

"Sex Pistols" By Nationaal Archief, Den Haag, Rijksfotoarchief: Fotocollectie Algemeen Nederlands Fotopersbureau (ANEFO), 1945-1989 - negatiefstroken zwart/wit, nummer toegang 2.24.01.05, bestanddeelnummer 928-9665 (Nationaal Archief) [CC-BY-SA-3.0 (http://creativecommons.org/licenses/by-sa/3.0)], via Wikimedia Commons.

"Elvis Presley stripped to his waist after escaping from a fan riot, during the concerts performed in Jacksonville, Florida between May 12-13, 1955." Florida Photographic Collection. Wikimedia Commons.

"Don McLean" By Herbert S. Gart, management (eBay item photo front photo back) [Public domain], via Wikimedia Commons.

"Beach Sunset in Cuba" By Aaron Escobar, 21 March 2007, Wikimedia Commons.

"Puente Colgante de noche, ciudad de Santa Fe" (Argentina), July 3, 2006.

"Sky Tower" (Auckland, New Zealand) at night, from Viaduct Basin, by Miguel A. Monjas, April 3rd, 2005.

1. THE HONEY THING

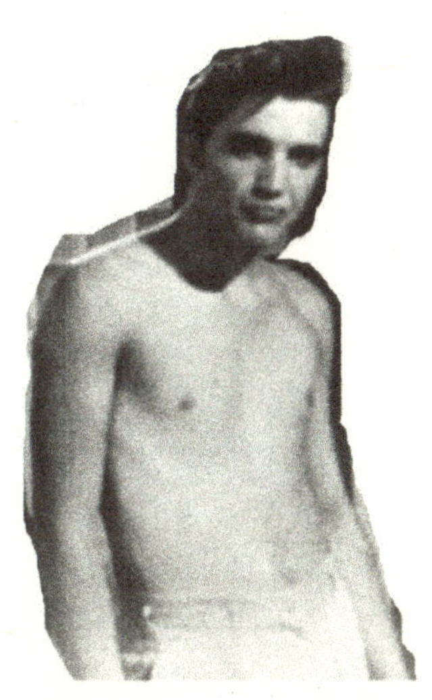

There's Someone in My Head but It's Not Me

That December, everywhere in Rajasthan,
in Uttar Pradesh, instead of Ravi Shankar,
I hear *Dark Side of The Moon*,

a buzzing from the touristic ruck that Pink Floyd
will perform impromptu on the beach,
New Year's Eve, which brings

every pseudo-hippie-dopehead-fuckup
zonking around Maharashtra or Karnataka,
in search of enlightenment on a dollar a day,

to Goa where, of course, Pink Floyd doesn't show,
but *I'm* there, wrapped in fringing
cotton, a spiritual purple, to greet

the year, the sky a mosquito net
of forty thousand stars,
with my best friend Sharlene,

whom I first met last week in Varanasi,
and we decide it would be really fine to sleep
under those stars on pure sand, which won't

be gritty, won't shelter biting fleas, because
it's *magic* sand, and we're with two guys
with great skin, Rain Dance and Flower,

jabbering to one another in Dutch,
trying to work out the logistics—him-her
him-me her-me him-him, but I've detached

from my body, became pure mind,
one with the glass-grazed sky,
so who cares if I'm with

Rain Dance or Flower, because
our bodies are mirage and there's enough love
along this edge of the Arabian Sea

to encase a very large whale
like the one we discover in the inevitable
daylight, down the beach,

where the town-folk have come to stare—
women with kohl-lined eyes
—the whale, washed up onto the sand,

even more exotic than strangers,
its chewed viscous carcass, chinked torso,
very very dead.

Political Homicide

The bullet of happiness hits me;
I memorize how happy feels.
My blindfold's on
to deflect any defects.

You seem on the up and up, so
I fire back with kisses
like with so many lovers before.

Balls of supernova gasses cook
under my feet.

I become the person
different from my idea of me,
like Szymborska, different
from my idea of her, making
collage postcards:
one, a picture of a kitten
hanging from a hot air balloon,
a funny verse
on the back.
I beg you to be kind.

I turn away, and think,
with me,
a lot of love
will mean a lot of blood.

A Cathedral of Affection

Your cathedral of sound—
explodes only in my ears,
in mono,
in stereo,
any noise will do.
The way you do it in the shower—
sing along with *baby I love you*,
the oomph of *woa-oh oh oh*.
I challenge you to hit the high notes,
give me some handclaps,
a little Leon Russell on the piano,
Darlene Love to back you up.
Sing with the feistiness of the Ronettes
—their Washington Heights fight.
Your other fans don't tingle on your lips.
You sing this way for me,
your bad girl,
your dancing girl,
your girl to end all girls.

Motown Marvelous

Twelve years old with a boxful of Motown 45s and an imaginary boyfriend named Randall, I decide he writes novels and looks like Clark Kent in the Lois Lane DC Comics series (though he can't fly to save his life). He wears black jeans like mine, but without the Clorox I use, washing out the color to make them cool. I lie in bed for hours, my hand rubbing my breasts, as I rehearse Randall taking off my cat-eye glasses to tongue-kiss me after he tells me he never realized how beautiful I am: a page from True Romance. The need to remove the glasses to be beautiful is essential, a fast path to fabulousness. What's best, he lives right here in what my local paper calls the City of Aspiration. I aspire to overwhelm him with my authentic sexual self, though I'm still vague about the details.

One day, my friends and I are sitting around my room, the Marvelettes on the turntable, as we debate whether we could ever telephone a boy. Laughing at the idea, I grab my pink Princess and dial BE 4-5789. A man answers with a voice like the background fabric of the paintings sold at the art fair on Saturdays three streets down. "Wait," my wrong number says, when it looks like I'm going to do a quick fade, "I believe in fate, don't you?" "Meet me at Eddie's?" He asks, all sweet with suggestion. I've told him where I live and that's the nearest ice cream place.

Then, Lizzie and Christine, miming a slow dance, do a dip back as I slap down the phone, throw myself on the floor, laughing so hard I hurt. When I dial the number three days later—after an imaginary fight with Randall—it rings and rings.

Any Sense You Had in the Morning
Is Gone When the Day Is Done

Growing rich in their sleep,
too many guys
don't know my favorite
horizontal mambo moves.
I don't want it like a machine,
needle in a groove.

I want a sweetheart like you,
with a sweating heart that
comes from loving me the most,
a scream that begs for open G tuning,
no fretting,
no pressing the wrong strings.

The money thing: okay
you don't have it—
not so grand, but
let me show you
what a cheap date I am.

Ray Charles said he could
only sleep in one bed at a time.
I'm not sure
that was true for him or is true for you,
though I bet
you'd be so fine,
you'd do the honey thing
so well, you would make
my brain swell—

Lo, Lola, Lolita…

On Sunday, one can get *there*
from *here* on the IRT line
but can't return, a logical
impossibility, except in New York City,
where track repair is infinite and rectitude
is flimsy.
My first memory of the subway—
I'm not even legal:

a skinny man with acne-scarred skin,
brown teeth leans in on me as I hang on
the shiny white metal pole,
my hair curled to my waist,
Miss Ten-Year-Old Innocent,
his hot stink-breath on me, a travesty,
according to Mother, bulking up
frog-like to wedge him
out of the way.
Two persistent adults
struggle over me and I think it's funny;
they take it seriously.

I know what he's doing.

I want my brittle power
over my glowering mother.
I see a clear future
where she'll spend
a lot of days in just that way.

Absent Consciousness

Capitol Records thought the Beatles had no future
in America. Their *Somnambulant Adventure*
photo shoot—

on the *butcher cover*: white bloodied smocks,
mock carnage of raw meat,
false teeth. Like *in the middle of a dream*,
glass eyeballs,
naked doll babies, their heads decapitated.

After its release, every copy
of the *butcher cover*
of *Yesterday and Today* was recalled
and pasted over—replaced to
avoid any possible controversy or undeserved harm.

Somnambulant adventures—
controversy and harm.

When I buy a copy, I want to
peel away the top layer, but
minimize the damage done.

High-Heeled Boys

Explain to me
the difference between a saxophone
and sex.

The music of both is so powerful
it surpasses registers of my voice.

I need you to explain to me
how some people lose their ideals,
make profits from dreams,
become the authorities.

I need you.

I need your sass.
Rebel lover with a cause,
that street spirit
lips and hips.

I need you.

Don't worry about the thinning hair.
If you don't get snapped in two by the money,
my ambitious honey,
you'll have a round of my applause.

You're playing that thing—
unaware of the power you have.

With Me, You Can Get What You Want

Want—as in to crave, as in I *want* your conga,
your maracas, your bracelet around my hips,
my bedroom man, as in, you're my favorite
flavor, your footloose lips. You lead to
blood-stained hands (see metaphor);
you're my London Bach Choir,
what I desire. As in who said you can't
get what you *want*? As in, require.

I met you when I wasn't young,
but I was young enough. *Want*—
is *want* the lust, and love the feeling,
or do I *want* to love, or love to *want*?
I'll take the whole cherry red cake,
the whole 50-amp fuse.

Blackbird

Momentary lindy swing—
your sandpaper skin upon my face.
Disparate breaths.
A muddy fountain

flows under the bridge,
to the territory where we've been
flecked with the usual mutual sins,
including those of omission.

We rock and roll
in our mud-lined nest on the ivy creeper.
I raise my chin and you flute a note,
and we have mated for life.

As if a thousand blackbirds sigh,
fall out of the sky
—their broken wings,
coiled sensibilities—
when we move apart in the wetness.

Because the Night

In concert, when Bono slips on a lyric
and sings *love is a blanket*
instead of *love is a banquet,*
both are accurate—similarly to
reaping both wool and lamb from sheep.

That night, I visualize you,
but can't reach or find you,
so I smash my fist
through the window
of my bedroom's door;
glass sliver slices my wrist.
For hours in the hospital I forget,
then, as the doctor stitches the wound—

your love finally becomes my sheep.
When scars are kissed, licked
with warmth and sustenance,
love is blanket and banquet and then,
who among us *isn't* a rock star?

White Rabbit

With a long-haired boyfriend, she rolls
on the bed next to the window,
entangled in the cord of her computer.
The air is hot, thick.
They must be in love; they're laughing.

I look at her body,
at my body through thirty years.

We are practically sitting next to them
on our hotel terrace in Bologna.
In their two rooms in the building across,
clothes drape every doorframe.
I see myself, my first apartment.

She sings along with Italian rock,
Stevie Nicks, and Jefferson Airplane:
Tell 'em a hookah smoking caterpillar...

"She's doing something to her legs
with strips of cloth," you tell me.
All four of us, getting ready to go out.

The next morning, her green shutters
stay closed. Is she tired of our company?

By late afternoon, she's at her flowered
plastic table, rolling cigarettes,
her windows wide open.
You hum along to Jefferson Airplane
on your iPod.

I accidentally drop cigarette ash into my drink,
gasp for air,
laugh, and she comes to the window.
The air is a hazy mirror of lazy time.
She looks at herself through thirty years,
lifts her hand and waves.

A Jamaican Sailor's Forbidden Love

Holed up in my bedroom playing hooky from school, we play the Kingsmen's disc at 33 RPM, instead of 45 RPM and listen really hard to "Louie Louie's" forbidden words. The lyrics are impenetrable—so we unspool the mental lexicon of the ones we know, try to fit them to the sounds. In my girl-crowd, shock is sexy, subversive, cool.

Words can lead us astray—Robert Kennedy, Attorney General, receives a letter from a parent who wants abrogation, annihilation, thinks the lyrics are obscene. Hoover's Feds can't decipher them, though they spool through their mental lexicon too. Could *on the ship* be *hey you bitch?* Is *Me see Jamaica*, instead *she's got a rag on?* They investigate for two years. The record is *unintelligible at any speed*; the extra notoriety spurs sales.

A sailor sings a ballad about his distant love: it's sung using one large mike to save money but it muddies the words. They seem suspicious (to us, delicious), warrant investigation, these menacing verse-choruses, *dirty sounds.* The Feds wonder if the obscenity is accidental. A serious matter, this rock and roll. What the Feds can't see: Jack Weinberg, Berkeley Free Speech Movement, about to say, *we don't trust anyone over thirty*, anyone that old is poised to become complete poison.

My Love Ain't No Stranger and He Ain't Got No Car

You sing, *love is a stranger in an open car*,
and tell me, "let's be unrestrained
in our derangement, pretend
not to know each other—
see how that works out."
Well, if you're a stranger,
might you also be a serial killer,
and do both unwrap into
equally deranged fantasies of fetish
chains?

Which do I prefer—
you as my pill, you as my pillar?
One day, love is my Dexedrine,
It helps me focus on one thing, you.
Next day, you give me a Valium,
and I curl up and sleep by you.
With both, I neglect work, and lose life
for pill-tranquility. Passing out on the Valium,
I find your pillar, and scratch my elbow
on the concrete and plaster. What's left
is that delectable discretion of the skin,
to sing: *And I want you*
And I want you...

It's true—we're all just sexual *cicatrici*,
scars and debris.

Face the Setting Sun

The road transects a terrain
of well-ordered young grapevines,
where we, in turn, take snapshots
standing on the weedy tangle at the border
against the clumped pebbled green.
This unfrequented island, Sardinia.

At the *nuraghe*, we stop
to touch 3000-year-old gray stone,
warm from the day's sun,
stoop in the low entryway to survey
a beehive-shaped room.
Rocks have collapsed into piles—
even palaces diminish,
this ruin opposite the circle
where the village's patriarchs used to meet.
No people now, and if there were softness,
we could sleep with pleasure
in the heat. But there's only archaeology
and dry brush.

Later, in the quiet, sitting on one of the low
seats of the circle,
you smoke your *Toscano* and smile at me.

It's the first time I notice you've grown old.

2. MOOD ALTERATION

Kissing Cold Air

You should have warned me love would not be
a closed-end dream of walking under water
but overdriven
amp, riff and flatted fifth, and a treble
wah-wah pedal's exaggerated pitch.
I wasn't prepared for the fuzzed sound.
Love is a sunburst Stratocaster,
slung across your back, a robust
gun, mondegreen, soramimi.
Take a right-hand guitar,
turned upside down, re-strung
for left-handers. What this gets—cries of love,
scarves that don't cover
hidden scars. What Jimi Hendrix got
was death by Vesparax.

And if I had been plucky,
love might have raised me an octave
instead of *fast deepening into black*.

Days of Haze and Cloud

It was twenty-five years
before Stevie Ray Vaughan detoxed
(he started in with drink when he was seven),
sober for three before he strapped
himself into a Bell 206B's
last seat, going to Chicago.
At thirty-five, he dreamed
he was at his own funeral and the next day
tears in the street—the pilot
hit the side of a slope,
making his sobriety moot,
dead so young, you could see the sky crying.

Cocaine, booze, cocaine, booze: you'd say
we don't always choose if we live or die—death's
a petulant mistress—and what's the point
if it's a long snooze instead of a brilliant time?
A better band, Stevie said,
always meant a better stash.

Life dealt underhanded to this
no-Leave-It-to Beaver Stevie.
But what if there was no dense fog,
no hill,
no crash?

The Story's Always the Same

That year, I almost didn't leave for Ohio.
You'd found us a place to live—
they wouldn't allow my dog.
Up the hill from the plain
under the Division Street Bridge.
We wouldn't have to see the mills.

A photo of you backlit at night
by steel fires,
the molten metal ladled below,
twenty-five miles along the Mahoning.
Black Monday,
fifty thousand jobs lost. Before
the Works all close for good.
Think Union
—you pasted those stickers
on every Cadillac you found.
My dog never did trust you,
your works, your heroin,
knew which side was buttered bread.

You called the landlady
so I'd go.
Charmed her. Turned slag to sinter.
"A little dog.
We'll carry her in and out."
We did. Charm
spoils quickly.
Here, the incense scent
of sweet grass.
There, a residue
in yellow-orange air.

Let's Pretend It Didn't Happen

Correction:
Kermina Suzani
is not the name
of the guest with green hair
depicted opening night
at the Antiques Fair
in Weekend Outings,
but the style of carpet
shown to her right,
more colorful than the rest,
hand-dyed, more red carpet
than the guest.
Just in from the copper city
—Bukharan—
backed with cotton,
this many-storied warrior
of the silk road
is not for sale, though
the guest may be.
(We're being snide—this
is unlikely
and not verified.)

The photographer who took
the photo displayed
at the show was not,
as originally stated,
Julia Margaret Cameron—
it obviously was dated
later and made by Henry,
her youngest son.
Julia's was placed elsewhere,
as now is the person—in rehab—
who wrote
last Sunday's column.

A Willow in Autumn

I'm losing sleep over the vanishings.
My shin is gone one morning.
Yesterday, an ear.
Like missing persons—
I must wait twenty-four hours
to file a report.
There's you, diminishing too, in parts.
Does a lover's love not fade away?
An elbow over there
by the radiator.
I'm watching carefully.
The dog's chewing on a piece of you
as if there's no tomorrow.

The Only One She Found

In the end, there's room for only one
in the small blue house,
a petty treason, husband killing.
There's the good wife and the aberrant wife
—her devious life, dressed
in the wrong clothes,
don't care if you hurt me some more.

She does care, does not mean to belong to him
like a pair of his boots.
Too easy to confuse abuse with love
and the other small blue house
where a gang of men
rape her when she's eleven,
but, that's a different story—
don't care if you abuse me again.

She does care. When she runs
away from all she's got, he finds her,
tries to drown her, to wash off the stench
of disobedience.

She does not know
there will be better friends
in prison than she's ever had.

She stabs him in his sleep—
the bread knife
goes in quiet and quick.
Sometimes she sees double
from the times he hit her in the head,
sees two victims, two knives, two deaths,
two wives.

The Crowd That Was Sedated

Only ten people show up to hear the Ramones in 1976 at their first big performance outside of New York. They are in Youngstown, Ohio and that explains it, a town with not enough energy left to face a three-chord band, even when it's in your face for the taking. This happens not long before the city's Sheet and Tube factory finally shuts for good, though when the Ramones later sing *Nothin' to do, nowhere to go*, they mean London shut for Christmas, not Youngstown. London, as always, reopens after the New Year. The Ramones are there to fuel the British-American punk rock scene. Youngstown never fully recovers from the shutdown.

Each Ramone rejects individuation by wearing the same leather and denim, a Neo-Leo Strauss version of punk, though Joey Ramone is heavily liberal (Johnny Ramone is hardcore right). I wear leather and denim too. The Ramones are from my high school and later when I'm in Youngstown, I feel I'm on a parallel track with the band, and that showing up in London will lead to success for me. But no matter how many times I go, success never happens.

Here's where we also diverge: Dee Dee Ramone, writer of a lot of their songs, is a heroin addict for much of his life, overdoses at fifty. Joey Ramone, the band's other prolific writer, credited with "I Wanna Be Sedated," is into serious drinking, until he quits and dies of lymphoma. Johnny Ramone, who doesn't like the band to record songs about drugs, dies of prostate cancer. Tommy Ramone is the most-together member of the band. He's replaced by Marky Ramone in 1978, just before "I Wanna Be Sedated." No one's last name is really Ramone; no one and nothing are really related. Tommy and Marky are the only ones still alive. Like me. Safe for now from the ultimate sedation.

Volcano Girl

In 1933, Kiyoko Matsumoto, a student at Jissen Girls College,
jumped into Mount Mihara, an active volcano. This led to a
copycat suicide epidemic at the site.

Your friend doesn't yearn for you like you
yearn for her

and the department store roofs
are blocked now to those who leap—
fences, guards—diminishing choices.

To erase this life,
disappear into the burn—Mihara's embrace,
its furtive lava.

You don't know the hundreds who will bury
their dread to follow you,
fall to their gloaming
...trying to make it back?
Back into the womb of the world?

One suspended moment
of regret,
a threatened bird—a *tori*—night heron flying
into the sun.

Midden of Human Remains

Eleven crushed to death in the forward rush,
the press of eight thousand
gathered for a concert,
the maximum packed
into standing-room space by promoters
until momentum became broken glass,
those who fell, unable to scream.

Two fifteen-year old friends
were the youngest buried.
Bodies, contused bodies,
the confusion of bruised breath,
too few open doors.

Barbarians (the Chicago Sun-Times)
numbed their brains on weed, chemicals
and Southern Comfort.

Everybody—all of us
(Pete Townsend, performing that night)—
we're all bloody responsible.

Not for the getting wasted,
just the waste: the stain
of coats, shoes, and gloves of December
on the plaza, a wave pattern of those
lifted off their feet,
morning of disbelief—one more
psalm of mourning.

Synonyms of Fiction

No day's grief is ever as brief as
what I hope for. One dry eye
batting open in the a.m., too wrecked

to know it's safe to put both feet on solid
ground. What's so sturdy
anyway about a squalid oak board

floor, now finally breaking up
(can it be your slut
poking her fingers through),

once covered by an inch of wayward
pump water? If I run my finger down
the horizon of each slat, I can feel

flood-soaked curls. They brought in giant
heat machines to blow,
to dissipate the dirty water,

after the flow stopped. I mean,
this wasn't New Orleans and so, the boards
were dried and saved,

neatly sanded over. Still, at each first light,
diffusing the lace, I think of what was lost
—the nonsense of your absence.

I pleaded, *please try to love me*,
so don't blame me for your pedestrian sin;
when it happened, I wasn't even thirty.

Collide

Quench
your resistance, your lack
of eye contact
when I say I love you. As if the junction
between us would vaporize—
this perturbation
of soot and spark.
As if I didn't try to ramp
it up until the inevitable failure—
no surprise, a year to reach
clear underperformance.
Where rats store their fear,
the memory of it sticky
in *your* brain, as you lick
your lips and hesitate
when I ask where is this going.
As if we're not already lying
cattywampus on the linen,
an energy shortfall.
Maybe there isn't anything
but bad connection, cramp, exploding
splices, imperfection
in three dimensions.
No oomph, except the smash
of will, mine against yours.
As if you weren't already ready
to take your volts and bolt.
As if I could contain the helium. As if
it weren't the end of the world,
this joke—that I could win
you over.

Tomorrow Isn't to the Right

The lunar eclipse begins.
Night and day commingle as we
awake for this diminished shape.
Reddish texture
emerges slowly—apparition.

Earth's shadow has its reach.
You reach for me, commingling.
Downstairs in the dark

a small crowd gathers at the corner.
In here, warm, the sky is easily
visible, its coincident solstice.
What always makes us notice—
conjunction of several specialties.
Love at times a solstice too, so greatly
distant, this sun,
this earth.
Lovers,
then a happiness that eclipses
each of our self-sufficiencies.

We won't live to see another
such cosmic alignment.
Reach for me now, again,
while we still can.

He Needs a Wealthy Woman

Getting dressed is a task
and not because of fashion's flash.
Those five, seven, nine items
she could retain in the brain,
shrunk to one.
She lies in bed,
mourning,
choosing among the rings of hell.

I lie when I try to soothe my old friend,
say (1) sooner or later,
it's like everyone's mourning,
besides (2) there's no hell;
we deal with nothing but nostalgic spasm.
The first's not true,
I hope. I'm the only one of the two of us
left with hope.

This I remember: her moonwalk
and spin in her Jheri-curl perm;
she could do it like the best.
She had the dance,

but now she doesn't have the steps,
her days run out, the rest
to be spent shuffling in a waxed linoleum
palazzo, days sub-zero
in their pleasures. Inside,
the atmosphere's fake-warm,
all else is gone—only institution,
medication, breath, and frown.

And the only thought holding her
is, he's not as cold as the ground.

No Way Home

The talk, metalliferous, that comes
with false concern from him enables you
to taste amalgam in your teeth.
His don't worry, he's-my-brother heaviness
downshifts your face, shoulders,
because you know his peace love, peace love
mother ship has circled the sewer drain.

You'd like to mesh a finger
into his brain, but, this needs to cease because
you don't have the heart for poetic justice—
the lock, stock, carbs—you don't have
the watermelons, garbanzos,
mutual funds, the Kolinsky mink.
You'd like to stalk off, to off him
and all the other dewlapped generators
of politico-economic world catastrophe,
give him enough well shots for a chance
he'd rot in hell. Look at that, you'd say,
the sassafras, the hash you've made of life's
questions. He won't have any answers.
No lodestone. No way home.

You Are Nowhere When You Swallow Pesticide

I meet you here after eight years,
for one more round, with hope
the yellow birds on the walls
will finally warble and look real.

I've got *a head full of pesticide.*
It's a crowded club,
a cocktail carnival.
Why do you drink...'til you're blind?
Just a singer at the baby grand, no band.
I'm trying to decipher
the difference between past and future,
luck and love.

We are still nowhere.
What you have to tell me,
you say it like you're right:
you don't like my drinking
5-inch heels
lipstick
weight
onion-breath
sour humor
red hair
and how I wobble on the marble
as I stagger out—

Murdered by a Melody

"So you want to learn to play the acoustic guitar,"
he said to me, all teeth and spark,

the second string band guy
whose fingers could do anything

in the dark of my bedroom, so thrilled, enthralled,
impaled, slain I became. He was the guy

I'd dreamed of—turnkey love. The tune
of screaming more-more-more lit a metallic silver

path to heaven. To death? Well... to love,
then I fell on the way up,

a clunky sofa pulley-hoisted on a frail rope
maintained only by me. I was tone deaf

in the about-to-change world,
moments before HIV, PCP, 2C-B,

CDSC, the I want my, I want my, I want my
money money money money money honey!

club drug decade—and did I mention a Gulf War?
Not him—he changed his song,

left for Boston and his MBA degree.
Listen, it was 1980

and Reagan got elected and very quickly
everything went down the crapper.

It's All I Love It's All I Hate

You're disheveled flash on beveled
glass and you eat too much meat.
I am placing this in evidence in a poem—
worms within stones—in lieu of
getting a gun, in lieu of being a shrew,
in lieu of purging my urges, in lieu of drinking
so hard the bottle aches.
Though I don't trust the musk,
my history of mass-
produced sex, with you I am getting better
at being worse.

I read about a woman
who loses her nose to cancer,
has to wear a metal shield.
Here are the lumps, here are the scars.
I am your metal shield. No,
you are *my* metal shield. I am your frightened
animal kneeling in the snow amidst
scatterings of bones.

Besotted with your art, though my mind
is clotted with rot,
this century has not yet gobsmacked me.
See, you can't tell me a lie
I don't already know
about this nausea,
this desire,
this viscid, vicious, quivering snout of love.

Smack, Crack, Hack, Anything but You Jack

A hundred cigarettes of regret
spiraling smoke from the tip—
vagary of hidden addiction, more
pathetic than me, the not getting over it.

Under a blue umbrella at that burnt-coffee
café you loved more than you loved me,
sheltered from the busy street, I loved you
a hundred squared.

Sneak thief of hearts,
your mind, a hundred unmined diamonds,
all willing to be cut more than you cut me.
Your funeral eyes.

We smoked our final cigarettes together.
I visited my grave.
You loved the white lady, your bitch mistress,
tapped your cigarettes in the powdery

stuff you loved more than you loved me and
though I tried a hundred times
You go back to her
And I go back to—

Bizarre Love Triangle

She's crying, does not want their crazed days to be over.
They have to be. I tug on him to end this instability,
behavior too extreme—
my frantic pulling up of bedding
again, to smell for remnants of her perfume.
Her heels, like narrow-muzzle
guns, echo up the stairs to where I'm standing,
looking down; I'm
shot through with a bolt of blue.
This triangle seems bizarre,
can't be that most mundane
of pains from routine heat of flesh and entanglement,
a cliché. Is he what he seems?

Murmuring voices
and the scents of Frangipani
mixed with weed from the sheets—I wonder
which of us feels
most betrayed.
This popular theme, this game, this crowded
trampoline of love.

I Can't See My Own

I don't want to be a hibernating lover
asleep under bridges of regret,
old themes feasting upon me, an abyss of ice
and ire. I have to turn my back on you,
grieve the seminary of disillusion.

You have skeleton eyes.

I grieve the eyes.
The world has graveled,
spilled out of you, naked, gray,
as you have spilled out of me.
I grieve every avalanche and vagrancy.

I grieve the music bar and grill where
we hung our hats, its muted greens
—closed two years now. I grieve the hats.

Nothing's left but cool silence,
shimmer of a silver mirror.

Now, May and dismay—I grieve the mirror.

Forget About Your Used to Be

You walked this passage so many evenings
in the gray of rough-

awakened moon. Ghost-bright store windows,
their skinny manikins with black ruched

fabrics, elegiac. Peddlers breaking down their carts,
waxy fruit of fake handbags,

pelle intrecciata. Taxi drivers
weaving their way through streets,

a concerto of horn,
the stink of garbage at the dirty curb for pickup,

plastic bags chewed open by dogs.
So many times with torn black stockings,

you walked, sagged and bent,
up the street to the *dirtiest hotel in America.*

You didn't see the sequence of bad nights
before the skin's sad and meager thickness

dissolved in disappointed expectation.
Skin, your sole protection from the madness of others.

You had a destination—
so many times it was a bed of scorn.

It's Over and I'm Walking Out on You

On a canopied mountain path
of the vermillion Inari shrine
in Kyoto,
shrine to god of rice and wealth,
you trek through the snaking
torii gates when a monkey
jumps upon your back,
mutant monkey strapped to you,
luscious you. A breed half the size
of a man stops you dead
as no one else can, hairy
clothespin claws hanging on,
a steel-trap grip. You pause to debate
with self what to do with the extra
weight, wary of attack
by the teeth of its rubbery pink snout.
The monkey jumps off and sits,
idol at your feet for a time,
rebounding to mount as you move
forward stop forward stop
monkey on off on off—
You have two clacking wooden
sticks, reach out with one to tap
the monkey who springs to run
from the graspable you,
frightened primate speeding

away from whatever we do,
we're going through it together.

I'm leaving because
I admit to being a monkey, but
you're a man who carries sticks—

Monkeys and wooden sticks don't mix.

Divorce Song

Vacated love, this eternal
dead season,
pitiful bored thing, dissolves

even further
—the dog's already gone—
into a fight over money, what
belongs to whom.
It's a loaded gun. I'm so tired
of looking at your face!

         And you at mine.
Take the damn entertainment system
and the sofa, already. Leave me alone.
Fine, leave me the loan. So like me to
try to placate the enemy.

Your mind's digital archive
stores my every committed sin;
over that, there's no true prevailing.

For months after, as if it's heroin,
as if we couldn't stop if we wanted,
dizzy, eyes tightly closed—
we dance the hard-luck fuck.

3. DO A SONG ABOUT IT

Relax

When did *I love you* become dirty?
When did *I love you* become a radio edit?
Relax don't do it they sang.
I could

blank the song,
bleep it,
resample it,
sing over it,
backmask it,
skip it,
distort it,
do an echo scratch, or
get the robo voice—quick—get the robo voice—

When did *When you want to come*
become dirty?
When did *When you want to come*
become a radio edit?

When Frankie Goes to Hollywood
sang *Relax*, so what if it
referred to sex? It went to number one.

But "I love you" follows words like that
and it's clear this time
you didn't want to hear it.

Symptoms of Lovoholic Addiction

Transformation into tight choreography,
all stepping in the same pattern with melody,
precision and amazing
grace straight out of the church,
the sex-injected amen lived here.
Then it dared to shift to something harder,
a dance closer to despair.
This was the snake of heartbreak
at Detroit's Fox Theater.

What could have remained: the disks
on Kissin' Radio, the KYSN countdown,
the Funk Brothers' duplicated instrumentation.
Motown desegregated
white ears through the soul-pop blend
—it *got* blues and gospel
—it *got* loss, the drowning,
 then redemption.

But redemption slipped away—with just a note
on the door, Motown moved to LA.

We were transfigured by the love,
before the police raid on a *blind pig*
rocked the city for five dazed days.
Before the barricades. Before the troops.
Before three teenagers were killed
at the Algiers Motel by the police.
Before a flicked cigarette lighter in an apartment
led to a 50-caliber machine gun blast.
Before the dead were as young
as Tanya Lynn Blanding, age four.
Before 12th Street, Grand River Avenue
were laid waste by burning.

Wailing and Howling at a Dry Moon

Pyrotechnic jets sparked fountains of stage gerbs
a hundred milliseconds
after Great White began to sing "Desert Moon."
It seemed part of The Station's show,
magic light with hard glam
headliners. But there was a grunge of heartbreak,
a lack of sprinklers,
gouts of *fire like a heavenly light*. Inflamed egg-
crate high density acoustic soundproofing,
polyurethane insulation foam in the nightclub
walls and ceiling was engulfed. The billowy sea
of black smoke in the munge meant
stampede and crush. A front door blocked
by falling bodies led to the trampling rush.
Those not led out to rescue, entire constellations,
were crunched by fire. This, too,
is rock and roll, the saddest part.
C'mon now, I know where we can go.
Nobody ever dreams of
what can happen in less than a heartbeat:
a hundred beats,
a hundred blue and white memorial lights,
red balloons,
a hundred expelled breaths.

Respect

What I want,
you don't got it.

Your plaintive sludge
is drone doom,
death gothic.
I need
some up-tempo

so I'm taking care of business
—taking my leave
of your thick lyric.

Your love,
or whatever you call it,
is a sieve,
your personality's
a scrub brush.

You never
scrambled eggs for me,
can't give

even a drop of yourself,
even a glass of cheap wine,
even a drink of sink water.

Shakespeare's Sister Doesn't Want You

She arrives with Abbie Hoffman as bodyguard
and 600 micrograms of LSD
hidden under her fingernail.
Grace Slick, gorgeous rocker chick,
raven-black hair, fails in her plan to spike
Tricky Dick Nixon's tea at a White House lunch.
Anyway, alcohol is her truest drug of love.

She sits under a tree in Marin County,
drinks wine,
reads poetry.
Sure, there were successes.
But, after a couple dozen rehabs, she'll be
all lumpy stuff with lines.

So many people live on propaganda,
like in her song, "Crazy Miranda."
Oh never mind—she's not your kind.
This is how it was
and is.

And if Tricky Dick, full of paranoia,
had been toyed with, had toyed with LSD,
would we be remembering Watergate? The secret
bombing of Cambodia?

Would any lives have been saved?

Ambrosia

Doo-wop first appears on wax in 1954—"Never," sung by Carlyle Dundee and the Dundees from LA. Later, everyone thinks: street corners, tracks and tunnels, subway platforms in the Northeast and industrial Midwest. Group harmony joins *doo-wop* with *sh-boom* and *oop-shoop* to create a variant on the hard *doo* and soft *wah* of *doo-wah*. There's blended second tenor and baritone; a child-castrato-falsetto; bass on the bottom end, imitating instruments; melisma-lengthened words as in gospel—*o-o-only you*; the lyrical convulsions and sometime heavy background beats with dialectical four-chord progressions. The usual disillusionment and love expressed in the lyrics, nonsense syllables and no-nonsense promise and desire, crest in the slowed-down sounds of the harmonies, like The Flamingos' remake of Dick Powell and Ruby Keeler's "I Only Have Eyes For You." The last true *doo-wop* hit is "Lover's Island" by The Blue Jays, featuring Leon Peels (one of many groups named after birds), which peaks at number 31 on Billboard in 1961. "You're Gonna Cry" is on the flip side and, years later, when it's an oldie, but new to me, I do cry, as I do after every trip to Lover's Island, despite the promise of *never*—a broken promise, I know, of a place where *love never grows old.*

Blank Beauty

The countdown year to my divorcing you,
Sid Vicious learns the bass guitar
by staying up one night,
a good ear tuned to the Ramones,
and plenty of methamphetamine.
He's fast, like the pet hamster, a biter,
for whom he's named.
Benders count more than playing well—
a lesson from the seventies. In distress
from our most recent spree, I vomit
in front of you as if to say
our marriage isn't selling itself.
The Sex Pistols model the New York Dolls
for bad attitude, vomit in airports
in front of the press.

In New York, Son of Sam is caught for killing
six and wounding more, with a .44.
He says a demon possessed
his neighbor's dog,
who commanded him to rampage.
While he's loose and unidentified,
we scratch fate's eyes
in our car in Cunningham Park in Queens
by having sex, one final bout of mischief.
The media, most of all the nearly-bankrupt
New York Post, stalk the killer.
He's not as photogenic as Vicious.
Mama Vicious in her local paper says of Sid,
he's not going around murdering people
though, later, there's the Nancy thing;
a knife, small wound, she bleeds, she dies.
He dies.

We die of our small and grander wounds.
Everything in those years was doomed.

Demolished World

Who doesn't feel the rifts,
the fractured vocalizations?
Joyce Carol Oates wrote of his voice,
as if sandpaper could sing.

With a pickup group at Newport,
an electric set, there was outrage, booing
—Dylan broke from folk.

And I broke from a husband.
People sleeping in broken beds.
No one could repair me, I thought—
a cracked
Humpty Dumpty.

But, like the singer from Dinkytown,
there's clash and crash—
his broken neck vertebrae—injury,
then it's fixed.

When the hound dog
howls and the bullfrog croaks,
it's the way they voice inevitability.

Because they're broken,
Because they think
everything is broken.
Because the dog and the frog can't change.

Devil in Nylon Hose

You can cover a hot song, but
you can't keep a hot song down—

not Big Joe Turner's glorious boogie woogie
twelve bar blues shout, "Shake, Rattle & Roll"
which burned the R & B charts for months
before Bill Haley and His Comets
made the lyrics beige.
Way you wear those dresses,
the sun comes shinin' through…
was reduced to
Wearin' those dresses,
your hair done up so nice.

I get over the hill and way down underneath
vanished under a blanket—
the lyrics turned to waxed placidity.
The acrobatic sax gave Haley
a hit
despite the toned-down sex.
It moved us white girls over
to uptempo race music;
Turner became a rock star too.

Big Joe roiled gin joints
without a microphone,
the way he began in the 20s mixing
drinks in a club, 300+ pounds of barman,
rocking when the idea moved him.
His roughed-up song
retained its joyous clamor.
Coming in at #126, it was Turner's sexy version
that made Rolling Stone's list
of the 500 Greatest Songs Of All Time.

Maybe he's still cabareting somewhere,
clubbing until mornings.

My Twin Bed Only Houses One

My Tuscan terra cotta pot
arrives cracked, its lid intact.
It's often like that,
this planet of contrary,
supposedly made-for-each-other parts.
There goes this week's bean soup.

You've moved to the muted West,
my fire-worked chrysanthemum,
to play L.A., a muted
counter-move in this incompetent,
discrepant love. It's a conundrum

why so much substantial
and essential is mismatched;
the lid needs the pot—
though we could argue
who is the lid, who is the pot.

The Endless Chorus

Bono and Mick Jagger sing a duet
at the Rock & Roll
Hall of Fame 25th Anniversary Concert.
Big-lipped Mick is so jittery and skinny—the song's
more juiced than when Bono
recorded it with U2.

Together, each sings better.
It's how, with you, though I never said it,
I became an improved version of me.

Bono wrote the words for Michael Hutchence,
lead singer of INXS.
Right before his suicide, he left a voicemail
—*Michael here. I've fucking had enough*—

then hung himself with a leather belt;
in the snap, the buckle broke.
Bono's lyrics are the words he wished he'd used,
the intervention he wished he'd made,
before his good friend killed himself.

But no matter how many words,
how smooth the talk,
isn't there's always more we wish we'd said?

Give Me Money

Greed, sure, the best things in life ain't free—like Alan Freed figured about the free stuff: *you can give it to the birds and bees*, blacklisted from broadcasting in the 50s for taking payola, drinking himself to death at forty-three, broke by then and bitter. Or Dick Clark, who decided love wouldn't pay his bills, cooperating with the cops.

Widespread racial animus towards the southern black geniuses of early rock and roll can't be historically erased. BMI, their record company, had to pay in secret to get airplay they otherwise wouldn't have had.

Bribery prosecutions, the bigger money behind them, were meant to go after rock and roll itself. Rock was no passing fad, but a delinquent juvenile, a Larry Williams-style bad-boy, blamed for the moral decline of teenaged girls. (*Cretinous*, Sinatra said about the songs.)

Rebel rock and roll, in its tight black jeans and Ducktail, stuck its tongue in our mouths and the feeling of disaffected defiance was what we'd been waiting for. It refused to die young. It refused to die beautiful.

Down Lonely Street

Up and back, up and back,
marching to Sousa, scratchy brass notes
falling out of the cheap
speaker at her waist,
the neighbor who has never spoken to me
flips the switch today, to early Elvis:
Just take a walk down lonely street
To Heartbreak Hotel.

Okay, I planned to marry him,
like so many girls before me—
the sultry early Elvis, before his gospel,
added chorals,
pills and other adult disillusionments,
not to mention death.

I twitch with nostalgia
over that rockabilly balladeer's
loose and twisty-hipped promise of sex.

My neighbor says, "I preferred the crooners more,
now I don't remember their names."

His sex was emphasized by a rumored Coke bottle
stuffed in his crotch.
Feverishly, I fixed on Ed Sullivan,
gatekeeper of childhood,
wanted only to see
the rock, the roll
of Presley's televised pelvis.

The Day the Music Died

It was a faulty heater, a four-seater,
a freezing winter in an Iowan cornfield.
It was a lost coin toss for a seat on a Beechcraft Bonanza V-tail,
a newly installed Sperry F3 altitude indicator.
The pilot couldn't read it, thought he wouldn't need it.
It was a storm—

Charles Harding [Buddy] Holly performed
at a packed Surf Ballroom in Cedar Lake. 1500 fans
drove through mess and squall,
to hear him and the others—Ritchie Valens,
The Big Bopper and more.

It was a charter to Moorhead, Minnesota, the next destination.
Buddy breathed with relief to find the pilot and plane.

It was a rush, a spurned bus, so frostbitingly cold.
The Big Bopper had the flu;
he asked Waylon Jennings, Buddy's bassist,
for the second seat.
Ritchie Valens had never been in a plane so small,
flipped Tommy Allsup for the third.
Three rock and rollers and their pilot
tossed out dead from the plane.

It was a real show stopper.

Dancing in Broken Heels

Like the theremin, I'm easy
to learn and difficult to master;
I confess
my irritating portamento,
my oscillating tone.
Things got all messed up—
you wanted swoon from me,
but got wanderlust.
From you I wanted
the fullness of sousaphone
and got squandered lust.

I'll bet you thought you could play me,
betray me. I didn't let you
touch me;
you wanted the Russian in me,
you wanted a woman in *tacchi alti.*

Even Lenin needed lessons in music,
electromagnetism. There's that theremin again—

I spackled on slippery red lipstick,
slipped into sparkly red heels
—back in the meet and greet market.
I got all dressed up,
adding to the mix
a dash of Romani
Mariachi. Tell me—baby,
in this place
are there *any* men with souls?

Withered Wallpaper

Like Dickinson with her *Impregnable of Eye*,
Don McLean wove a song around *albumen*.

Rancid is another word
quirky in his song,
like *vulgar* or *sulfur*.

Yolk of the egg in albumen
referred to the dawn;
his neon fuchsia syllables
sung the way slippery thread-memories
of an old love affair
are often worth more than the love.

They Come In Sweet and They Go Out Cold

This pattern of endings—lace
upon the glass panes,
frost
inevitable it seems,
then the glance bent backward,
recantation of the thrill.
That day in the train station
when we first meet. Cinder eyes
—ashes and slag.
Static of announcements,
indecipherable audio,
the woman at the flower stall
(red carnations)—
I know even then
it won't be too long
until I place the blame for us
on my sore shoulders

though you'll write the song
about it. Months later,
I hear it on the radio.
It's raining.
They predict a long cold December.

NOTES

The following, in page order, is the music that stimulated the creation of the poems in this manuscript. Other groups may also have recorded versions of these songs.

The Honey Thing:

  "Brain Damage," Pink Floyd, 1973
  "Dog Days Are Over," Florence + The Machine, 2008
  "Baby, I Love You," The Ronettes, 1963
  "Beechwood 4-5789," The Marvelettes, 1962
  "Gasoline," The Dead Weather, 2010
  "Gothic Lolita," Emilie Autumn, 2006
  "I'm Only Sleeping," The Beatles, 1966
  "The Low Spark of High-Heeled Boys," Traffic, 1971
  "You Can't Always Get What You Want," The Rolling Stones, 1969
  "Blackbird," The Beatles, 1968
  "Because the Night," Patti Smith, 1978; Bono, 2009
  "White Rabbit," Jefferson Airplane, 1967
  "Louie Louie," The Kingsmen, 1963
  "Love Is a Stranger," Eurythmics, 1982
  "Grow Old with Me," John Lennon, recorded 1980, released
posthumously 1984

Mood Alteration:

  "Purple Haze," The Jimi Hendrix Experience, 1967. The quote in the final
line is from a description of a purple haze in Dickens' *Great Expectations*
  "The Sky Is Crying," Stevie Ray Vaughan, recorded 1985, released
posthumously 1991
  "Youngstown," Bruce Springsteen, 1995
  "Let's Pretend It Didn't Happen," Mike & the Mechanics, 1991. Partially
found poem
  "Not Fade Away," The Rolling Stones, 1964
  "You're All I've Got Tonight," The Cars, 1978
  "I Wanna Be Sedated," Ramones, 1978
  "Volcano," Beck, 2008
  "Baba O'Riley," The Who, 1971. The Riverfront Coliseum incident killed
eleven people in 1979
  "You Cheated," The Shields, 1958

"Collide," Leona Lewis / Avicii, 2011
"Hyperdrive," Jefferson Starship, 1974
"Nothing from Nothing," Billy Preston, 1974
"No Way Home," Richard Durand, 2009
"We Are Nowhere and It's Now," Bright Eyes, 2005
"Killing Me Softly," The Fugees, 1996
"L.A. Song (Out of This Town)," Beth Hart, 1999
"Back to Black," Amy Winehouse, 2006
"Bizarre Love Triangle," New Order, 1986
"Turn My Back on You," Sade, 1988
"Confessin' The Blues," B. B. King, 1965. Dedicated to Mistress Kris, formerly of The Nuns, murdered in the Hotel Carter in New York City, 2007
"I'm Gonna Leave You," Dusty Springfield, 1966
"Divorce Song," Liz Phair, 1993

Do a Song About It:

"Relax," Frankie Goes to Hollywood, 1983
"What Becomes of the Brokenhearted," Jimmy Ruffin, 1966
"Desert Moon," Great White, 1991. The Station nightclub fire killed a hundred people in 2003
"Respect," Aretha Franklin, 1967
"Crazy Miranda," Jefferson Airplane, 1971
"Lover's Island," The Blue Jays, 1961
"Pretty Vacant," Sex Pistols, 1977
"Everything is Broken," Bob Dylan, 1989
"Shake, Rattle & Roll," Big Joe Turner, 1954. Bill Haley's version was released later the same year
"Sleeping Single," Roxette, 1988
"Stuck in a Moment You Can't Get Out of," U2, 2001
"Money (That's What I Want)," Barrett Strong, 1959
"Heartbreak Hotel," Elvis Presley, 1956
"American Pie," Don McLean, 1971
"Bad Luck Heels," DeVotchKa, 2011. *Tacchi alti* means high heels in Italian
"Tapestry," Don McLean, 1970. *Impregnable of Eye* is from Emily Dickinson's "I dwell in Possibility"
"Boys Will Be Boys," Gear Daddies, 1988

OTHER ANAPHORA LITERARY PRESS TITLES

Michael Connelly
By Stan Schatt

East of Los Angeles
By John Brantingham

Death Is Not the Worst Thing
By T. Anders Carson

Folk Concert
By Janet Ruth Heller

100 Years of the Federal Reserve
By Marie Bussing-Burks

River Bends in Time
By Glen A. Mazis

Interviews with BFF Winners
By Anna Faktorovich, Ph.D.

Compartments
By Carol Smallwood

Printed in May 2019
by Rotomail Italia S.p.A., Vignate (MI) - Italy